MOUNTAIN MISTS

A Story of the Virungas

by Evelyn Lee

Illustrated by Paul Kratter

Soundprints
Where Children Discover...

For the mountain gorillas, with hopes for peace in their homeland and a continued dedication for their survival — E.B.L.

To my loving family, Joel, Marshall, and Tia. This book is also dedicated to Dian Fossey and her life work with the mountain gorillas. Special thanks to Andy Kratter — P.K.

Illustrations copyright © 1999 Paul Kratter.
Book copyright © 1999 Futech Interactive Products, Inc., Phoenix, AZ 85018.

Published by Soundprints, an imprint of Futech Interactive Products, Inc., 353 Main Avenue, Norwalk, Connecticut 06851.

Book layout: Diane Hinze Kanzler
Editor: Judy Gitenstein

First Edition 1999
10 9 8 7 6 5 4 3 2 1
Printed in Hong Kong

Acknowledgments:
Our thanks to Charles Horton, Curator of Primates at Zoo Atlanta, for his curatorial review.

Library of Congress Cataloging-in-Publication Data

Lee, Evelyn.
    Mountain mists: a story of the Virungas / by Evelyn Lee;
illustrated by Paul Kratter. — 1st ed.
            p.   cm.
    Summary: In the Virunga Mountains of Africa, a young gorilla travels with her family group, eating and sleeping in the safety of the jungle.
    ISBN 1-56899-785-X (hardcover)   ISBN 1-56899-786-8 (pbk.)
    1. Gorilla — Juvenile fiction. [1. Gorilla — Fiction.   2. Zoology — Africa Fiction.
3. Endangered species — Fiction.   4. Jungles — Fiction.   5. Africa — Fiction.]
I. Kratter, Paul, ill.   II. Title.
    PZ10.3.L514Mo   1999
    [E] — dc21   99-19981
                                                                              CIP
                                                                              AC

MOUNTAIN MISTS

A Story of the Virungas

by Evelyn Lee

Illustrated by Paul Kratter

The
Nature
Conservancy®

Early one morning in the Virunga
Mountains of Africa, the first rays of sunlight filter
though the branches of a hagenia tree to a thick
tangle of green forest below. Garlands of mosses
drape down from the branches, and ferns and
orchids spring up from its bark. A cool, white mist
climbs the hillside as a nine-year-old female
mountain gorilla awakens in her well-hidden nest
of vernonia branches. Soon, eleven more black,
furry bodies rustle in the leaves for the start
of a new day on the ancient volcanic slopes.

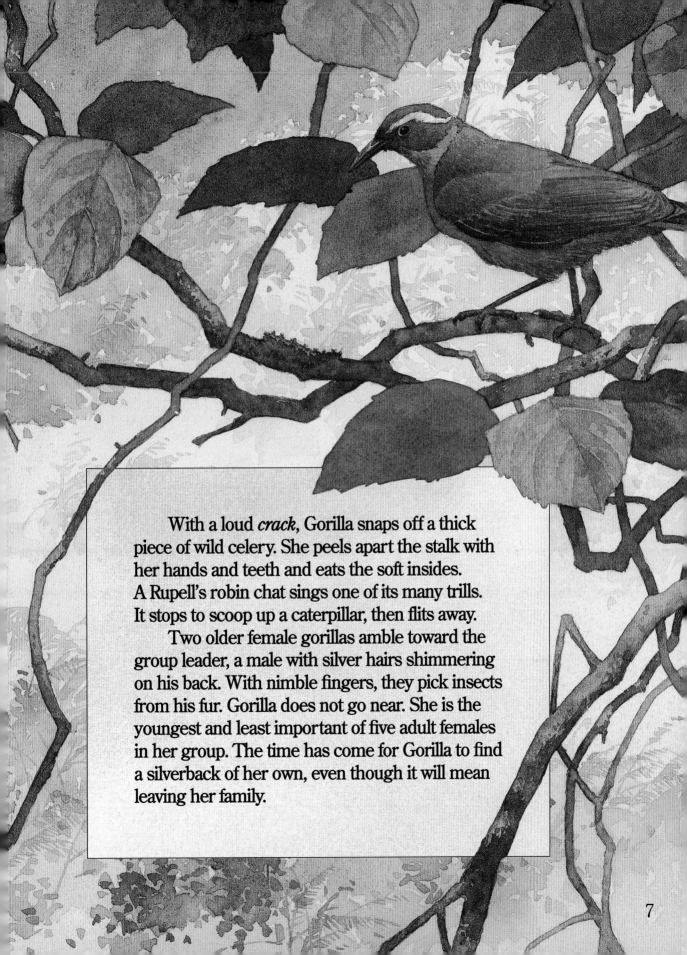

With a loud *crack*, Gorilla snaps off a thick piece of wild celery. She peels apart the stalk with her hands and teeth and eats the soft insides. A Rupell's robin chat sings one of its many trills. It stops to scoop up a caterpillar, then flits away.

Two older female gorillas amble toward the group leader, a male with silver hairs shimmering on his back. With nimble fingers, they pick insects from his fur. Gorilla does not go near. She is the youngest and least important of five adult females in her group. The time has come for Gorilla to find a silverback of her own, even though it will mean leaving her family.

All morning, Gorilla trudges with her group through the dense understory. As she stops to taste some nettles, the ground begins to shake. Overhead, golden monkeys and spot-nosed guenons screech and swing through the trees. Soon a large elephant plods past on a muddy trail.

When all is quiet again, Gorilla hears a sound coming from up the ridge. It is the hooting of a lone silverback. He has lived by himself for three years and is ready to start a family. Gorilla listens carefully. Her group's big silverback hoots back a warning to stay away.

At midday, Gorilla and the others bend thin branches of young hagenia trees and bedstraw into circular nests on the ground. Gorilla has barely settled down to sleep when she hears a rustling noise close by. She sits up, very alert. It is only a bush pig, settling down from its night of grubbing for tree roots in the mud.

Gorilla falls asleep. Around her, bees hum and dip into the pollen of yellow hypericum flowers. A little bee eater darts through the branches and snatches a bee with its beak. High overhead, a martial eagle circles in the sky with large outstretched wings, looking for a meal.

Barely an hour later, a band of L'Hoest monkeys comes clattering through the trees and fills the forest with loud calls of alarm, waking Gorilla from her rest. A startled golden cat slinks through the branches with a newly-caught warbler. It swiftly disappears into the leafy canopy.

Stirred awake by the noise, a large eagle owl swoops into the open. It hopes to snatch a bird or mouse for itself. Gorilla stiffens at its unexpected flight.

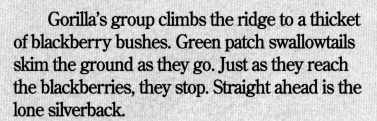

Gorilla's group climbs the ridge to a thicket of blackberry bushes. Green patch swallowtails skim the ground as they go. Just as they reach the blackberries, they stop. Straight ahead is the lone silverback.

Gorilla glides forward. The old silverback follows. The lone silverback charges until he is a few feet away. He stops. Both silverbacks stand stiffly on all fours, with hair tufts fluffed forward and lips sucked in tightly. Everything is as still as can be until finally the lone silverback stands up on two legs, hoots, and rapidly strikes his cupped hands against his belly. He drops to the ground and the old silverback lunges toward him. The lone silverback is no match. He runs back. The old silverback stares sternly at Gorilla and returns to the group, with Gorilla very close behind.

15

That night, as Gorilla sleeps,
tree hyraxes leave their den and scuttle
through the trees. They call to each other with loud
creaking noises and scratchy sounds that can be
heard for miles. A genet quietly slinks from branch
to branch, searching for food. In an opening,
a bushbuck grazes on grasses and leaves. When
the bushbuck hears the genet, it freezes, ready
to leap and run.

Two yellow-backed duikers also stand very still
at the sound. When they see the gray-spotted figure,
they whistle loudly. The genet dashes away.

17

Early the next morning, a loud crashing noise stirs Gorilla awake. The lone silverback has come back, bursting through the plants, trying again to find a female. A blackback herds the gorillas single-file down the ridge to safety. The old silverback stays to defend his group.

The two silverbacks bite at each other and tufts of fur fly into the air. Both are hurt in the fight. When the lone silverback leaves, Gorilla follows him. This time, the old silverback lets her go. As Gorilla and the lone silverback run through a tangle of vines, a frankolin scurries through the underbrush. The old silverback returns to his family.

Grabbing onto vines, Gorilla climbs the steep
ridge with the silverback that will protect her for
life. A Ruwenzori turaco runs from cover as the
two move past. On and on they climb. Finally,
Gorilla and her new silverback stop.

The silverback cleans a cut on his arm and
Gorilla watches. Then she looks high into the
trees. A family of black-and-white colobus
monkeys looks back at her. With its tail billowing
out behind, one parachutes down to a lower
branch where it sits to eat a handful of leaves.
Many others stay draped in the tree, their long
tails hanging limply to the side.

During the night, rain and thunder come to the mountain. Gorilla and her silverback hunch over in nests protected by tree branches. A porcupine moves slowly by. A bushbaby swivels its head from side to side. Its red eyes peer through the dark in search of food. As soon as it sees a moth, it swipes the air with lightning-fast speed and traps the fluttering insect between its palm and flattened fingers.

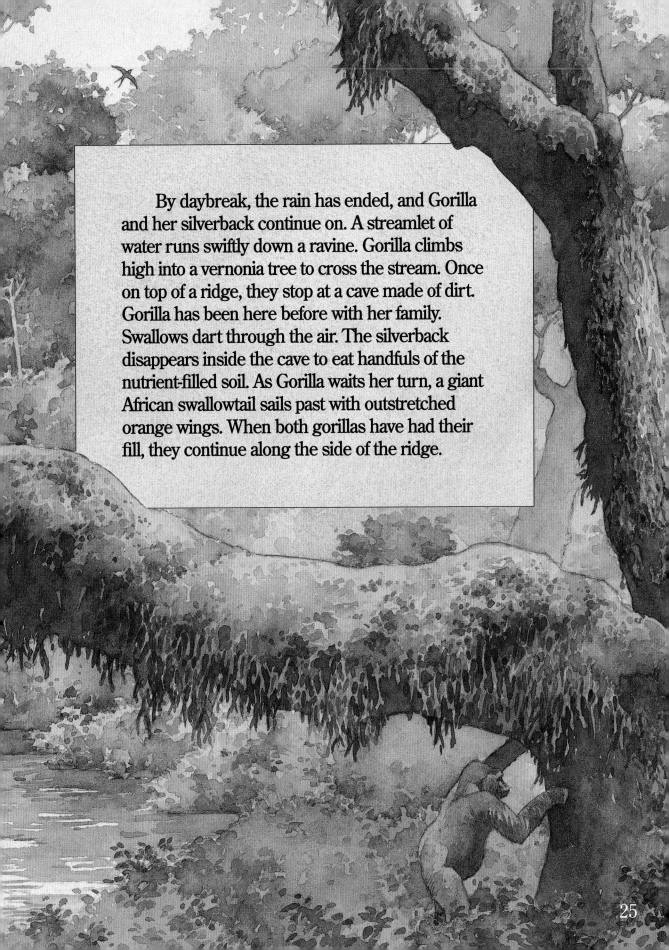

By daybreak, the rain has ended, and Gorilla and her silverback continue on. A streamlet of water runs swiftly down a ravine. Gorilla climbs high into a vernonia tree to cross the stream. Once on top of a ridge, they stop at a cave made of dirt. Gorilla has been here before with her family. Swallows dart through the air. The silverback disappears inside the cave to eat handfuls of the nutrient-filled soil. As Gorilla waits her turn, a giant African swallowtail sails past with outstretched orange wings. When both gorillas have had their fill, they continue along the side of the ridge.

Late in the day, the two gorillas are high in the mountain, where there are fewer trees. Tufted lobelia plants dot the ground. Gorilla stays hidden near a senecio tree and watches double-collared sunbirds flitting among the flower stalks. As the shadow of an auger buzzard slips past, the birds dart into woven nests.

Then, Gorilla follows the silverback down a different ridge, one that is new to her. She is leaving her family farther behind. She is now ready to explore a new part of the mountain, and perhaps to start a new family of mountain gorillas in the misty Virunga Mountains.

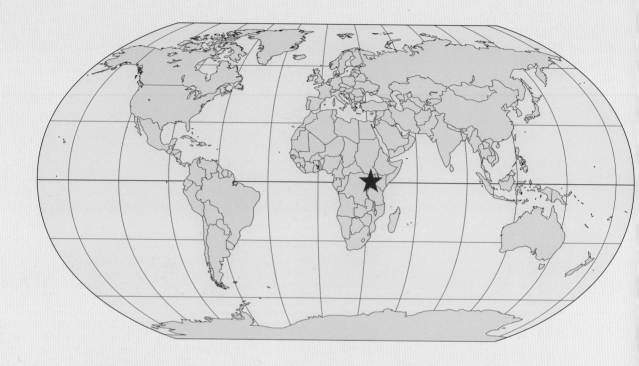

The Virunga and Bwindi Conservation Areas, East Africa

The Virunga Mountains run along the borders of three African countries—
Rwanda, Uganda, and the Democratic Republic of the Congo. Some 325
mountain gorillas live within the 160 square miles of parkland in the
Virungas, known collectively as the Virunga Conservation Area. Another
300 gorillas live separated in the Bwindi, or Impenetrable, National
Forest of Uganda.

Glossary

▲ African forest elephant

▲ Eastern black-and-white colobus monkey

▲ Hypericum

▲ Scaly frankolin

▲ Bamboo

▲ Fern

▲ Large-spotted genet

▲ Southern tree hyrax

▲ Bushbuck

▲ Golden monkey

▲ Martial eagle

▲ Spot-nosed monkeys

▲ Crested porcupine

▲ Greater bushbaby

▲ Red river hog

▲ Spotted eagle owl

▲ Duiker

▲ Hagenia tree with mosses

▲ Rupell's robin chat

▲ Vernonia tree

About the Virunga Mountains

More than 150 species of mammals, including fourteen primates, live in the Virunga and Bwindi Conservation Areas, but some stay at lower elevations than the gorillas. Bwindi is located in a very old valley and has nearly 345 bird species and several rare and remarkable butterflies.

Nowhere else do mountain gorillas exist. Once, rain forest extended between the Virungas and Bwindi and gorillas moved between the two areas. About 500 years ago, people destroyed part of the rain forest for farming and split the rain forest in two. The gorilla population was also divided.

People from Europe first saw mountain gorillas in 1902, when two gorillas were shot and killed for sport. Over the next twenty years, fifty more were killed or captured. In 1925, fearing a bigger loss of gorillas, the Belgian government that controlled the Congo and Rwanda started preserving the montane forest with a park on the Congo side of the Virunga Mountains. It was the first national park in Africa. In 1929, the government added land in Rwanda and three years later established the Impenetrable Forest Reserve in Uganda. More land has been added, right up to the 1990s, although big chunks of parkland were lost to farming in the 1950s and 1960s.

Illegal farming, cattle grazing, and the removal of bamboo and other wood for crafts and fuel is destroying the montane forest. Certain poachers have killed gorillas to sell their body parts for money. More recently, war between the Hutu and Tutsi groups of people has forced as many as six hundred thousand people to flee for safety in the mountain areas.

Before the war, in the 1970s and the 1980s, tourist trips allowed visitors from all over the world to see the gorillas. Money from the trips helped pay for patrols that protected the gorillas and the parks from poaching, farming, and wood-cutting. Trips were controlled so the gorillas stayed wild and did not catch human diseases, including common cold viruses, flu, measles, and mumps. Civil war has limited, or stopped, tourism and patrols but several agencies around the world, along with governments, are working to preserve the mountain gorillas and their habitat.

▲ *African golden cat*

▲ *Giant African swallowtail butterfly*

▲ *Mountain gorillas*

▲ *Auger buzzard*

▲ *Giant groundsel*

▲ *Northern double-collared sunbird*

▲ *Cinnamon-chested bee-eater*

▲ *Giant or tufted lobelia*

▲ *Ruwenzori turaco*

▲ *Garden warbler*

▲ *Giant senecio*

▲ *Wire-tailed swallows*

▲ *Mount Kahuzi*